T0134791

But God...
chose you!

Copyright © 2020 Ginger K. Buck.

All rights reserved. No part of this book may be used or reproduced by any means, graphic, electronic, or mechanical, including photocopying, recording, taping or by any information storage retrieval system without the written permission of the author except in the case of brief quotations embodied in critical articles and reviews.

This book is a work of non-fiction. Unless otherwise noted, the author and the publisher make no explicit guarantees as to the accuracy of the information contained in this book and in some cases, names of people and places have been altered to protect their privacy.

WestBow Press books may be ordered through booksellers or by contacting:

WestBow Press
A Division of Thomas Nelson & Zondervan
1663 Liberty Drive
Bloomington, IN 47403
www.westbowpress.com
1 (866) 928-1240

Because of the dynamic nature of the Internet, any web addresses or links contained in this book may have changed since publication and may no longer be valid. The views expressed in this work are solely those of the author and do not necessarily reflect the views of the publisher, and the publisher hereby disclaims any responsibility for them.

Any people depicted in stock imagery provided by Getty Images are models, and such images are being used for illustrative purposes only.
Certain stock imagery © Getty Images.

Interior Image Credit: Brittany E. Riggan

All Scripture quotations are taken from The Holy Bible, English Standard Version® (ESV®), Copyright © 2001 by Crossway, a publishing ministry of Good News Publishers. All rights reserved.

ISBN: 978-1-9736-8522-7 (sc)
ISBN: 978-1-9736-8523-4 (e)

Library of Congress Control Number: 2020902333

Print information available on the last page.

WestBow Press rev. date: 3/3/2020

WESTBOW
PRESS®
A DIVISION OF THOMAS NELSON
& ZONDERVAN

But God... chose you!

God's Story of Love in a 7-day Devotional

Ginger K. Buck

Illustrated by Brittany E. Riggan

In the beginning
God created the *world*,
BUT GOD showed
that wasn't enough;

when God, who is love,
in all His beautiful earth,
chose
to have *people* to love.

*In the beginning God created
the heavens and the earth.
Genesis 1:1*

God created
a *man* and a *woman*
to walk with and talk with
each day;

He gave them everything perfect
they ever would need,
BUT GOD allowed them
to *choose* their own way.

So God created man in His own image,
in the image of God He created him;
male and female He created them.
Genesis 1: 27

They chose to *disobey* Him
and they were afraid,
and hid from their Creator
that day;

they knew they'd done wrong
and caused a big problem,
BUT GOD is *love*
and He made a way.

*And they heard the sound of the Lord God walking
in the garden in the cool of the day, and the man and
his wife hid themselves from the presence of the
Lord God among the trees of the garden.*
Genesis 3: 8

Many years later
He sent down *His Son,*
to walk with and talk with
His people on earth;

He never did wrong
and was never ashamed,
BUT GOD chose to *save us*
through Jesus' birth.

For God so loved the world, that He gave His
only Son, that whoever believes in Him should
not perish, but have eternal life.
John 3:16

God chose Jesus
who never did wrong
to take our place
and die on the *cross*;

He didn't have to –
the angels would save Him –
BUT JESUS *stayed*
because He knew we were lost.

BUT GOD shows His love for us
in that while we were still sinners,
Christ died for us.
Romans 5: 8

Jesus *died*
so we could live forever,
BUT GOD knew
that wasn't the end;

Three days later
Jesus rose from the grave,
and because God chose to love,
LIFE WINS!

He is not here, for He has risen, as He said.
Come, see the place where He lay.
Matthew 28: 6

We've all disobeyed God
and don't *deserve* Heaven,
BUT GOD in His love
made a way;

If we *believe* in His Son,
that He died for our sins,
we will live with Him
in Heaven some day.

*And they said, "Believe in the Lord Jesus,
and you will be saved."*
Acts 16: 31

BUT JESUS looked at them and said,
"With man this is impossible,
BUT with GOD
all things are possible."
Matthew 19: 26

God Chose YOU
to be part of
His Story!

Put *yourself* in His story in this
7-day Devotional.

BUT GOD...

God created a perfect world
for His people to live in;
but when the first person disobeyed Him,
everything changed – for them and for us.

Life will not always be easy on this earth,
BUT GOD
is always the One we should turn to.

He chose to love us,
He is always with us to guide us,
and He always has the answers we need.

When we believe in Jesus as God's Son,
He teaches us in His Word how to live.
The Holy Spirit guides us
and He never leaves us.

...Chose You!

Over the next seven days,
put yourself in God's story.

Grab a notebook, your favorite pen,
and get creative!
Write your
thoughts as you Think,
prayers as you Pray,
and
the Actions you take
as you live out God's story.

God chose YOU
to walk with and talk with
Him each day!

So, let's get started!

Day 1

In the beginning God created
the heavens and the earth.
Genesis 1:1

In six days, God created a beautiful world with dry
land and seas, the sky with the moon and stars,
and all kinds of plants and animals.
Each day He said His work was good.

You can read the whole story of God's creation
in Genesis chapters 1 and 2.
Check it out!

Think about it

What are your favorite outdoor activities?
Do you like to camp, hike, climb trees, or go fishing?
Maybe you like to swim, ride horses or draw nature.

Talk to God

Thank God for creating such an amazing world
for us to enjoy. Today, write God a "thank you" note
in your journal for your favorite of His creations.

Action!

What can YOU do to take care of God's creation?
Maybe you could plant a flower, or walk your dog,
help a neighbor rake leaves, or pick up trash.

Choose one or two things to do this week,
then write in your journal about how it felt to help
take care of God's world with your own hands and feet.
Have fun serving the Maker of the Universe!

Day 2

So God created man in His own image,
in the image of God He created him;
male and female He created them.
Genesis 1: 27

On the 6th day, God created a man and woman
and placed them in His beautiful garden.
They were the first husband and wife.
God gave them many beautiful trees, and
He also gave them the choice to eat from
all of them ...
except for one.

Think about it

What do you think it would it be like to be one of only two
people living on the earth and to walk and talk with God?

Why do you think God gave them a choice to do right or wrong?
Why not just make them obey Him all the time?

Talk to God

Isn't it awesome that you can talk with the same God who
created Adam and Eve? He made you, too, in His own image!
That means that you can live forever with God.

Thank God that, of all His creation, *GOD CHOSE YOU* to love!
Thank Him that He gives you a choice to love Him, too,
and that He never leaves you.

Action!

Read Ephesians 1 & 2 written by Paul the Apostle
and make a list of all that God created you to be.
Ask God to show you how you can serve Him in a new way
because of these promises. Share this great news with a friend!

Day 3

And they heard the sound of the Lord God walking
in the garden in the cool of the day, and the man and
his wife hid themselves from the presence of the
Lord God among the trees of the garden.
Genesis 3: 8

God told Adam and Eve they could enjoy the fruit of all the
trees in His beautiful garden ... except for one.
God gives us all a choice to love and obey Him,
and they chose their own way.

Think about it

Have you ever done something you were ashamed
of and hoped no one would find out?

Adam and Eve were suddenly afraid of God,
because they had disobeyed Him;
BUT GOD is love, so He chose to love them.

Check out the first sin in Genesis Chapter 3,
and see what happened next to Adam and Eve.

Talk to God

Thank God for loving us, even when we disobey Him.
If you have disobeyed, talk to God about it.
Ask Him to help you make good choices.

Action!

In your Bible, read John 14: 15-31 where Jesus talked to
His disciples about the Holy Spirit who would be their Helper.

Think of something that you know God would want you to do.
Make a plan to get started, and write about it in your journal.
Thank God for always being with you,
and ask Him to help you obey Him.

Day 4

For God so loved the world, that He gave His only Son,
that whoever believes in Him should not perish,
but have eternal life.
John 3:16

Jesus increased in wisdom and stature,
and in favor with God and man.
Luke 2:52

Jesus was called "Immanuel," which means "God with us."
God came to the earth as a little baby to grow up and
teach us about Heaven and what it means to obey God.
You can read the story of when Jesus was born in the
first and second chapters of Matthew and also in
Luke's book, in Chapter 2.

Think about it

Why do you think God came as a tiny baby in a stable
and not a great king on a mighty horse to save the world?

The Bible says Jesus had brothers and sisters in His
earthly family. What do you think it would be like to
grow up with Jesus in the house as your brother?

If you met Jesus when He was your age, what kinds
of questions would you have liked to ask Him?

Talk to God

Thank God for choosing to send Jesus
to live on the earth like we do.
Ask God to help you obey Him like Jesus did.

Action!

Write a story about what it might have been
like to be friends with Jesus as a boy.
Do you think He would have been one of the cool kids
or would He have played alone and been left out?
Write about how Jesus knows what it feels like
to be a kid like you. Make a plan to be a friend
to someone who feels alone.

Day 5

BUT GOD
shows His love for us in that
while we were still sinners,
Christ died for us.
Romans 5: 8

Because of their sin, Adam and Eve,
and everyone born after them,
would die;
BUT GOD made a way
for them, and for us, to live forever.

Think about it

What was the greatest way that
God chose to show His love for us?
How does Jesus' dying mean we can live forever?
How does this verse show that we don't have to be
perfect to be forgiven and to deserve God's love?

Talk to God

Thank Jesus for taking your place and being punished
for your sins, so that you can be forgiven
and live with Him forever in Heaven.

Action!

Spend today being thankful for
the greatest gift we have ever been given
- the gift of forgiveness -
so we can live forever with God in His perfect Heaven.

Write God a thank you note to praise Him for all
He has done for you. Read Romans 5:8 in your Bible
and keep your thank you note on this page as a reminder.

Day 6

"He is not here for He has risen, as He said.
Come, see the place where He lay."
Matthew 28: 6

The greatest day in history was when
Jesus rose from the dead.
His friends thought He was gone forever...
BUT GOD
had another plan!

Think about it

How do you think you would have felt if you saw Jesus
die and watched as His body was placed in the tomb,
then you heard He wasn't dead anymore?
What would you have done next?

Talk to God

Tell God how grateful you are that because Jesus
rose from the grave, you can live forever with Him.

Action!

Read the story of Resurrection Day written by Jesus' friends
in Matthew 28, Mark 16, Luke Chapter 24, and John 20.

Put yourself in their places – how would YOU have felt
to be the first one to see His empty tomb?
Write your own story in your journal about what it would
have been like to arrive at the tomb and find it empty!

Day 7

"And they said,
'Believe in the Lord Jesus, and you will be saved.'"
Acts 16: 31

Jesus' disciples spread the good news to others that
believing in Him meant they could spend forever with Him.

Think about it

Have you decided to believe in what Jesus did for you?

Talk to God

Tell God how you feel about Jesus.
Thank Him for sending Jesus to live and die
for you, to take the punishment for your sins,
for rising again, and for making you a home in Heaven!

Action!

The last thing that Jesus said to His disciples when He was
leaving the earth was to go tell everyone near and far that
He is coming again!
If you believe in Him, YOU are His disciple!

Make a list of friends who need to know about Jesus.
Ask God to help you tell them and others about Him.
Share the great news about Jesus like His first disciples did!

Jesus said, "Behold I am with you always, to the end of the age."
Matthew 28:20

Printed in the United States
By Bookmasters